Dreams

Thorsons First Directions

Dreams

Soozi Holbeche

With love for Maggie Roberts.
May all your best dreams come true.

Thorsons
An Imprint of HarperCollins*Publishers*
77–85 Fulham Palace Road,
Hammersmith, London W6 8JB

Published by Thorsons 2001

1 3 5 7 9 10 8 6 4 2

Text derived from *Principles of Dreams*, published by Thorsons 1998

Editor: Louise McNamara
Design: Wheelhouse Creative Ltd.
Production: Melanie Vandevelde
Photography: Photodisc Europe Ltd., Emma Gilman.

A catalogue record for this book
is available from the British Library

ISBN 00 712 3531

Printed and bound in Hong Kong

Contents

Dreams

are the language of the night; a bridge between conscious and unconscious mind and body, body and spirit,

Introduction

Dreams since the dawn of time

Since the dawn of time dreams have fascinated mankind. Dreams from the Bible, from mystics, shamans and wise men, poets, authors, artists, scientists and psychologists have always been a source of creativity and knowledge and have been crucial to the development of civilization.

Ancient scripts and scrolls provide us with dreams and their interpretations that date back thousands of years. Clay tablets have been discovered, inscribed with dreams from Babylon and Assyria, dating from around 3000 BC. Early Indian, Egyptian and Chinese literature all describe dream messages and how to obtain them. In 2 AD the Roman soothsayer Artemidorous wrote a book on dreams, the Oneirocritica, which had a profound effect on all subsequent dream research. Homer, the Greek writer and philosopher, described the 'Gates of Ivory and Horn' through which dreams came. Dreams that were 'true and good' passed through the Gate of Horn, while dreams that 'deceived or deluded' passed through the Ivory Gate.

Dreams throughout history

There are countless examples of famous dreams throughout history. In AD 332 Alexander the Great dreamt that if he laid siege to the city of Tyre he would win it. Encouraged by this, he fought and won. Similarly, St Joan of Arc's dreams prompted her to fight for France against the English. Some dreams are not so propitious. Before his assassination, Abraham Lincoln dreamed of a coffin surrounded by weeping people and guarded by soldiers. 'Who is dead?' he asked. 'The President. Killed by an assassin,' was the reply. The assassination of President Kennedy was also predicted in many dreams, including those of a woman who telephoned the White

House the day before and warned that if Kennedy went to Dallas he would die.

Biblical dreams were believed to be direct messages from God. Some of the better known include the dream where Joseph saw an angel, Jacob's dream of angels climbing a ladder to heaven; and the vision of another Joseph, who dreamed he and his brothers were binding sheaves of corn in a field and his stood upright while his brothers' sheaves bowed in deference to him.

Shakespeare mentions dreams in most of his plays. One of his most famous quotes, from Prospero in The Tempest, *is: 'We are such stuff as dreams are made on.' Hamlet prays: 'To sleep; perchance to dream,' while Romeo dreamed: 'My lady came and found me dead ... and breathed such life with kisses on my lips that I revived and was an emperor...'*

Dreams as inspiration

An opium-induced dream brought the poet Coleridge his famous 'Kubla Khan' poem which begins: 'In Xanadu did Kubla Khan a stately pleasure dome decree ...' The novelist Robert Louis Stevenson found his dreams often inspired his stories, including The Strange Case of Dr Jekyll and Mr Hyde. Recently, Kekule, the German chemist, discovered the molecular structure of benzene through his dreams. When he reported his findings at a conference he said:

Let us learn to dream, gentlemen, then we may perhaps find the truth.

Henry David Thoreau wrote, 'In dreams we see ourselves naked and acting out our real characters, even more clearly than we see others awake,' while for Jung, the great psychiatrist, a dream was 'a little hidden door in the innermost and most secret recesses of the psyche'.

During the twentieth century psychological studies of dreaming, together with sleep laboratories and brain research institutes, have become increasingly popular. Dreamwork has now become an important part of psychological analysis. Books, seminars, television and radio programmes have all helped to move people away from the

assumption that dreams are 'only your imagination' or 'too much cheese for supper' and brought about the awareness that dreams have altered the fates of entire cultures and shaped the destinies of thousands of individuals.

Dreams teach, balance, inspire and heal not only the world's most original and creative thinkers, but everyone else too.

What Are Dreams?

The Penguin Dictionary of Psychology describes a dream as a 'train of hallucinatory experiences with a certain degree of coherence, but often confused and bizarre, taking place in the condition of sleep and similar conditions.'

Sleep is, in effect, an altered state of consciousness and for hundreds of years it has been the source of much speculation. Questions such as what was the purpose of sleep, what happened to the brain during sleep, and what caused sleep have long taxed the minds of scientists, wise men and philosophers.

Sleep clinics worldwide have discovered that, after colds, sleep problems are the most common health complaint. Lack of sleep,

especially dream sleep, can lead to mental illness, accidents and carelessness at work. Apparently, even if we miss two hours sleep in one night, we are sleep deprived and, in experiments with rats, sleep deprivation actually caused death.

We now know that during an average lifetime we spend approximately 24 years asleep and six of those years dreaming. These six years are longer than the average college or university course, but most of us dismiss our dreams as unimportant.

Rapid eye movement

In 1952, the creation of electroencephalograms, or EEGs, enabled researchers to make a breakthrough in sleep research. The EEGs showed that during sleep the brain had periods of activity as intense as when its owner was awake. This demolished the theory that the sleeping brain was simply resting. Through EEG the researchers discovered the connection between brain activity, rapid eye movement, now known as REM, and dreaming. They saw that REM occurred during dream sleep but not during non-dream or slow wave sleep.

Rhythms of the night

Our brainwave rhythms, or cycles, change during different phases of sleep. Scientists have named these rhythms alpha, beta and delta after letters of the Greek alphabet. Beta is the decision-making part of the brain we use when we are awake. Alpha is a slower, more receptive rhythm. Delta is the slowest cycle and occurs in profound sleep or under anaesthetic. The early alpha stage of sleep is so light that we may easily wake during it and insist we have not been asleep. It is during this phase that 'hypnagogic images' may appear. These are normally very clear and can include faces, landscapes, animals, dots or even shapes and blobs of colour.

We can stimulate these images for ourselves by pressing our eyelids gently with our fingertips or looking at brightly coloured images before going to sleep. After the alpha stage we gradually enter a deeper phase which brings overall relaxation, a slower heart rate, a drop in blood pressure and temperature. We then move into REM, or our first dream phase, and continue throughout the night to drift between deep, restorative sleep and spectacular, revelatory dream periods.

Today we know that REM sleep, or dreaming, begins about 90 minutes after we fall asleep and will re-occur every 90 minutes, approximately four or five times a night. During REM sleep, certain brain cells turn on while others turn off.

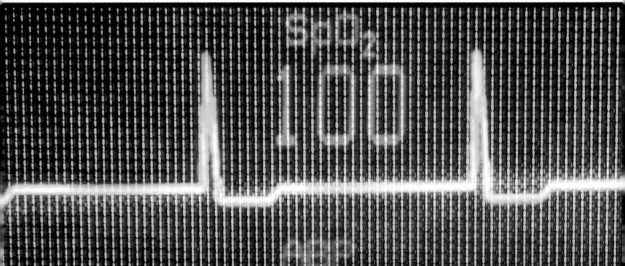

The cells that turn off release neuro-transmitters, chemicals that are crucial to attention, learning and memory, and this may be a reason why so many of us forget our dreams. (Although, interestingly, researchers also found that most people woken during REM sleep remembered their dreams in detail, while those left to sleep without interruption usually had no dream recall whatsoever.) At the same time as these cells switch off, the brain speeds up, blood pressure rises, breathing quickens and the heart beats faster. Despite the fact that our muscles relax, we may twitch, or even mutter and sigh under our breath. We are in another world, a self-created universe.

Episodes of REM dreams are separated by periods of calmer, deeper, non-REM or slow-wave sleep. Non-REM sleep shows brain activity, but statistically less dreaming. We spend approximately two hours, or 25 per cent, of each night in REM.

A sleep laboratory study of language students showed that students who had more REM or dream sleep were those who learned the fastest. Newborn babies spend much of their sleeping time in REM, which doctors believe is essential for their brain development. As we get older, our need for REM sleep diminishes and we dream less.

Dark and twisted visions

Cicero the Roman orator who lived from 106 – 43 BC described his dreams:

'There is no imaginable thing too absurd, too involved, or too abnormal for us to dream about… Do the immortal gods constantly flit about the lowly pallets of mortals…and when they find him snoring, throw at him dark and twisted visions… or does nature bring it to pass that the very active soul sees in sleep phantoms of what it saw when the body was awake?'

At the start of the 20th century psychologists, notably Freud and Jung, focussed much of their attention on dreams. Jung believed that dreams were essential to the discovery of the true self. While he examined dreams for what they might reveal, his early mentor Freud looked for what they might conceal. Freud also believed that a dream was a compromise between a person's need for expression and a need for rest. Therefore he sometimes called dreams the 'guardians of sleep' as well as the 'Royal Road to understanding the unconscious'. Both Freud and Jung have had a profound effect on our attitude to our dreams today and their dreamwork has coloured the world of modern psychology.

'I can never decide whether my dreams are the result of my thoughts, or my thoughts the result of my dreams.'

esult

dreams.'

'I can never decide whether my dreams are the result of my thoughts, or my thoughts the result of my dream

'I can n
of my t

'I can never decide whether my dreams are the result of my thoughts, or my thoughts the result of my dreams

'I can never decide whether my dreams are the result of my thoughts, or my thoughts the result of my dreams.'

'I can never decide whether my dr
of my thoughts, or my thoughts th

er decide whether my dreams a

oughts, or my thoughts the resu

'I can never decide whether my dreams are the result of my thoughts, or my thoughts the result of my dreams.'

'I can

In fact, once we learn to understand the symbols of our dreams we discover that they generally display a range of creativity and intelligence that most of us could not achieve even if we were to remain awake 100 years or more. So dreams can be thought of as a language, the language of the night; a bridge between mind and body, body and spirit, conscious and unconscious. Dream images are rich, colourful and explicit, and sometimes appear so completely real we believe that what we saw in a dream actually happened in life.

The writer D. H. Lawrence found dreams so real that, in a letter to a friend, he wrote:

'I can never decide whether my dreams are the result of my thoughts, or my thoughts the result of my dreams.'

What Can Dreams Tell Us?

What do dreams do?

- they mirror the day's events
- they can review and even solve unresolved problems
- they help identify emotional undercurrents we may not have been fully aware of
- they bring to the surface of our minds unconscious desires, conflicts and impulses
- they connect us to the past, present and future
- they provide us with amusement and pleasure
- they bring emotional balance
- they stimulate creativity and sexuality
- they can prepare us for the unknown
- they enable us to live out unlived parts of ourselves
- they can give us signs, reminders and warnings that may help us choose one path or another

In other words, dreams can heal, teach, warn and guide us. The objective and honest insight they give us, if we listen to them, can result in our waking up with a totally clear answer to what may have been, pre-sleep, an insoluble situation or problem. As soon as we begin to listen to our dreams, ask questions of them, and act on the answers and information given to us, we immediately draw on far more of our intelligence than before. This can empower us to do, change or become, anything we want. It is through dreams that we can tap into vast reservoirs of intelligence, memory and creativity that can empower us all to master life's challenges. As the Roman soothsayer Artemidorous said in his classic book on dreams, the Oneirocritica:

Dreams and visions are infused into men for their advantage and instruction.

Hundreds of years later, the famous psychic Edgar Cayce said:

All dreams are given for the benefit of the dreamer – would that he interpret them correctly.

Different Kinds of Dreams

'The dream is a spontaneous self-portrait, in symbolic form, of the actual situation in the unconscious.' Carl Jung

Dream images can give us vital information often unknown to our waking consciousness. As well as mirroring the events of the day, they also express messages that come from the unconscious to the conscious mind. These are presented to us through a variety of different types of dream which can be interpreted in many ways.

Recurring dreams

A recurring dream is one of the most important. It is like a message from the inner to the outer self which is trying to shake us awake to a problem or feeling we may have ignored, been unaware of or refused to deal with. Repetitive dreams often shock, frighten or humour us in such a way that we are forced to pay attention. A recurring dream will highlight unconscious frustration and resentment. Or it will bring to our awareness something that is wrong in our lives, but with an extra kick which, similar to a nightmare, releases a lot of repressed emotional energy.

A true recurring dream is one which is exactly the same each time and may repeat itself over a period of years – even from childhood to old age. If you have a recurring dream you may be stuck in some aspect of life and in order to move forward must both recognize and resolve the issues that are holding you back.

Nightmares

These are described by the Chinese as dreams of 'terror and dread'.
They can jolt us awake, screaming with fright or revulsion, with sweat
pouring down our faces and our hearts pumping with extra force as we
try to escape the threat pictured in the dream scenario. Nightmares are
different from dramatic dreams that may frighten us but do not jolt us
awake. Nightmares usually involve feelings of helplessness and a sense
of being out of control or at the mercy of external events and/or
people. Dream research shows that children suffer more frequently

from nightmares than adults, especially between the ages of three to six, and adult nightmares are often based on childhood feelings of powerlessness.

A study of pregnant women's dreams show that they reflect more anxiety and fear than dreams of other groups. Strangely, research also discovered that the more nightmares a woman had, the shorter her time in labour.

All of us, at some time or another, have had or will have a nightmare. Rather like a recurring dream, a nightmare is a call for help, healing and attention from the inner to the outer self. If we can recognize and deal with the underlying stress or problem we can also transform both ourselves and our lives.

To ignore a nightmare is similar to ignoring a flashing light on the road or on the dashboard of a car. It suggests we must stop, look, listen and take some kind of action.

Healing dreams

Healing dreams include those that warn us of impending ill-health, crisis or accident, diagnostic dreams which give us clues into the particular cause of illness, and dreams which do in fact simply heal us.

Prodomic dreams

A dream that warns us of possible ill-health is called a Prodomic dream. These often take the form of cars that run out of fuel or whose brakes fail. Buildings, machinery, clothing and vehicles are frequently used to symbolize the dreamer's body. Before we break a leg or undergo surgery we may dream of a torn piece of clothing, a collapsed building, a familiar piece of equipment refusing to function, or a storm on the horizon.

Dreams that predict the onset of a disease or heart attack often have a nightmare quality of war, earthquake, fire or famine, or show the dreamer wounded in the part of the body that later reveals itself as malfunctioning. Another health warning dream can be that of a policeman pointing out defective lights, flat tyres or a faulty exhaust on one's car. Prodomic dreams sometimes feature friends or colleagues with symptoms that actually apply to us.

These dreams do give us the chance to act before we become ill. If we record our dreams and review them from time to time we can also check for health warnings.

Many dream psychologists believe that a clue to your health in dreams is contained in the rate of activity in your dream images. When your metabolism changes from normal to too fast or too slow, your dream figures grow correspondingly over-active or inactive.

Diagnostic dreams

These dreams reveal the cause of physical problems, often when modern medical science has failed to do so. One nurse who had been sick for weeks without anyone being able to discover the cause finally dreamed of a shellfish that opened, revealing a worm that stood up inside it. An old woman pointed at the worm and said, 'That's what is wrong with you.' When the nurse awoke she was sure she had hepatitis A – a liver infection caused by eating shellfish from contaminated water. Her dream used the worm as a metaphor for the virus. Subsequent tests confirmed the diagnosis. In both Russia and America, many hospitals now investigate their patients' dreams to see if it is possible to correlate certain dreams with specific illness and disease.

Healing dreams

A truly healing dream is one when we go to sleep sick and, through the dream process, wake up healed. Inscriptions at ancient healing sites giving thanks to Asklepios, the Greek god of healing, testify that this type of miraculous healing has occurred since the earliest recorded history. Healing dreams will sometimes tell us exactly what to do; others may initially be more concerned with healing our psyche rather than our body. Illness, accident, rape or any kind of violence often causes feelings of helplessness and vulnerability. At these times any dream that encourages us to take action or control suggests that we have the power to overcome the situation.

Dreams in convalescence

After an illness, accident or surgery, healing dreams may initially replay the trauma, but later tend to comfort and soothe.

The dreamer may see or sense images such as warm hands stroking or massaging the body; meadows lush with green grass; gardens, plants, trees, flowers, buds opening; snakes that uncoil or shed a skin; seas that change from choppy to crystal clear and calm; the sun or sunlight pouring through a window or bathing the body in golden yellow light.

Other dreams which often depict recovery show the dreamer clearing or tidying a house, a chest of drawers or kitchen cupboards; or weeding a garden; choosing new clothes or uninhibitedly throwing off old ones. Sensual or sexual feelings in convalescent dreams also symbolize recovery and ultimate return to health. We can even invoke healing dreams to speed recovery during illness.

Prophetic, precognitive and telepathic dreams

Historically, 'dreams of divination' have been crucial to the lives of many people, predicting success in battle for Genghis Khan and Napoleon to Oliver Cromwell and Hitler. Jung and many others had terrifying, precognitive dreams about the Second World War.

- Prophetic dreams are usually concerned with future, more impersonal, community or even global issues.

- Precognitive dreams are usually more personal and give us a waking, intuitive hunch that suggests we do not catch the train, plane or bus that subsequently crashes, or that we keep our children at home from school for the day – as one mother did in response to a dream on the day of a dreadful school massacre.

- Predictive or clairvoyant dreams provide us with information about events of which we have no conscious knowledge. They are similar to a psychic reading and can only be truly assessed if the events prophesied subsequently take place.

- Telepathic or clairvoyant dreams put us in touch with and show us people and events not in our immediate environment.

These vary between personal and impersonal – telepathic dreams may concern a member of the family in trouble or they may present a clairvoyant image of a complete stranger.

Prophetic or precognitive dreams are fairly common, but most of us either pay no attention or dismiss them as fantasy. Usually they come with a gut feeling that compels us to act on what the dream said.

XVII

THE STAR

Compensatory dreams

Compensatory dreams restore our emotional balance by encouraging us to express sides of our personality we are either unable or unwilling to express while awake. These dreams show us an opposite side of ourselves, which can bring us sharply down to earth if we feel superior to, or critical of, others, or push us to stand up for ourselves if we lack self-love and acceptance. Another type of compensatory dream is the one that lets us explore an unlived part of ourselves that has been denied expression because of the life choices we've made.

Jung describes the recurring dream of an extremely difficult and argumentative woman. In this dream she saw herself beautifully dressed, arriving for a party. Her hostess greeted her at the door, saying, 'All the friends you know are here.' She then ushered the dreamer into a cow-filled barn. This dream helped the woman to become a little more humble.

Sexual dreams

Sexual dreams can shock, frighten, tantalize or embarrass us. They can cover the complete range of sexual experience, from straightforward joyful sex to masturbation, sex in unusual positions, in extraordinary and often public places, sex with familiar or famous people, sex interrupted by parents, heterosexual sex, homosexual sex and even sex-change as well as incest, rape and other forms of sexual violation. Instead of feeling guilty or embarrassed by such dreams, we should joyfully accept them – unless of course they are unpleasant, in which case we should delve into the underlying reasons for this.

  Dream research shows that both men and women who have frequent sexually explicit dreams they are uncomfortable with tend to repress or ignore problems in waking life – and not necessarily just sexual problems. Conversely, those whose sexual dreams are joyful, humorous and satisfying tend to face and overcome their problems far more easily. Also, people who openly discuss sexual dreams are often far more creative than those who are too shy or embarrassed to do so. Many therapists encourage sexually inhibited or frigid patients to ask for sexual dreams as part of their treatment. As well as revealing far more about a person's attitude to self, sex and sexual relationships

than discussion, dreams also allow
the dreamer to explore specific sexual
activities they may never have
tried before.

   People who appear in our dreams,
whether these are sexual or otherwise,
should always be interpreted as
aspects of ourselves first, despite
what other levels of meaning they
might also have. So whether we
dream of making love to the milkman,
the boss, a member of the Royal
Family, Brigitte Bardot or our next-
door neighbour, our dream mind is
pushing us to recognize and merge
with the qualities in us that are
symbolized by this other personality.
So as well as loosening up our
attitude to sexuality, dreams also
symbolize union with different parts
of ourselves. Even if we dream of
making love with someone of our own

sex, it does not necessarily mean we are blatantly or latently homosexual, but that we are reinforcing our own masculine and feminine energy and attributes. If a sexual dream partner repulses us, we must also look at why, and what in ourselves is similarly repulsive.

We can bring about sexual dreams by simply writing down, before sleep, what we would like to experience in the dream. If you wish to solve a sexual problem, write a few notes about the problem and your attitude to it first. Then simply write, in your own words: 'I want a dream that clarifies the source of my problem and how I may overcome it' or, for example, if you feel your sexual problem is your own inadequacy, write: 'I am embarrassed about my body being too fat, thin, tall, small, or whatever, so give me a dream that will improve my self-image.'

Dream lover

You can also use this type of exercise to ask for a dream lover if you do not currently have a waking-life one. If you do this, make a few pre-sleep notes about the kind of lover you'd like to meet in your dreams – humorous, kind, passionate, older, younger, tall, short, dark, handsome, beautiful and so on. Many of my partnerless friends have done this in disbelief and jest, only to find they had such a good time in their dreams that they stopped actively searching for a waking-life partner. Then, as soon as they relaxed and enjoyed the various people in their lives as human beings, rather than as prospective marriage partners, the man or woman of their dreams appeared on the scene.

Lucid dreams

A lucid dream is when we become fully aware of dreaming during the dream. We can then take charge of the dream and change it at will. In a pre-lucid dream, which is quite common, we have a vague sense of dreaming but not enough awareness to take some kind of action. Sleep clinics around the world are increasingly interested in lucid dreams and also in training dreamers to have them at will. Lucid dreams often include a sense of flying.

'Conscious' or lucid dreaming has been taught by many religions and cultures for centuries, from ancient Egyptian civilizations and so-called 'primitive' tribes to Hindu, Buddhist and Taoist religions.

Death and dying in dreams

Many people fear that the death of someone in a dream means that the person will die in waking-life. Yet death dreams seldom predict literal, physical death. Rather, they give us a nudge to change, to grow, to release, or 'die to' certain habits, relationships, emotions, as well as to old ways of living and perceiving life. So a dream of death is a metaphor for letting go of, or transforming, an aspect of ourselves, as well as an acknowledgement that something inside us may be dead.

Bill dreamt he was hammering nails into a wooden coffin which had his name inscribed on it. Anticipating imminent death, and worried about his family's future, he made a will. Months later, exhausted from the pressure of his job, which literally 'boxed him in', Bill remembered his dream and realized his workaholic attitude to life was nailing him into a position where there was no life, no room to breathe. Bill's dream had nothing to do with physical death but illustrated the death of his freedom, spontaneity and fun.

Often death dreams show a friend, neighbour or acquaintance being knocked over by a 10 ton truck, struck by lightning or falling off a mountain. Although these dreams can occasionally be predictive, they also mean we must look at what the person in our dream symbolizes, or represents, to us in our waking life. If we witness their death in a dream, we must question what needs to die in us, as well as our own attitude to death and the process of dying.

Dreams of those near death

Characteristic dreams of older people who are near death – from age rather than illness – are generally of loss: the loss of a purse, passport, wallet or handbag, for example. These all symbolize the loss of identity. Other common dream themes of approaching death are of funerals, journeys, seeing themselves in coffins or attending their own funeral, or of white birds, beautiful gardens, celebrations and flower-filled villages or houses. Change is also the significance of the death dreams of healthy children, which often include the death of their parents. Such dreams are connected to growth, discovery and moving from one phase to another.

Parents who dream of their children's death (when they are healthy) are often being reminded to let go of their children as they grow up. These dreams are sometimes the result of conscious or unconscious resistance to do so.

Dreams of dying children

The dreams of children on the verge of death are amazingly lucid. Katie dreamed she crossed a riverbed while her parents remained on the other side. When they tried to join her, she waved them back and walked into a beautiful garden where many other children were playing and dancing. Nine-year-old David, chronically ill with leukaemia, dreamed that he arrived on Earth by floating down in a balloon. A childhood friend, killed in a car accident three years earlier, then appeared and handed David a bunch of multi-coloured balloons. He said, 'When you want to use these balloons to float back to where we come from, I'll be waiting for you.' Suddenly David saw hundreds of children, all holding balloons, floating in the air around him. He awoke excited and happy at the thought of joining them. Both dreams enabled these two children to float away without fear, panic or pain when the moment of death came.

How to Stimulate Your Dreams

Although we all dream we often don't remember our dreams.
This may be because most of us grew up with the belief that dreams
were unimportant, a meaningless jumble of mental garbage, or
fragments, left over from the day's events and irrelevant to our waking
lives. But in order to use our dreams to enhance our lives, we must
first be able to value them for what they are!

The power to control, stimulate and remember our dreams begins with the simple step of deciding to value them.

If we were to do no more than impress upon our unconscious minds that we are really serious about dreams, and respect and honour the information they contain, the quality of our dreaming would automatically improve. If you have never paid attention to your dreams before, it may take one or two weeks of practice to obtain results, but if you use some of the following suggestions you will not only dream but also remember your dreams. In fact, many people have almost instant dream recall after reading one or two dream books. This is an excellent way to begin to set in motion your dreaming mind's co-operation.

Preparing yourself for vivid and memorable dreams

Most of us, whether healthy or sick, just hurl ourselves into bed when we feel tired, without any thought that a little 'sleep preparation' would ensure not only a good night's sleep, but also better dreams. The following suggestions are all extremely useful, whether you practise only one or two, or all of them:

- Eat lightly and less a little earlier in the evening than usual.

- Create a peaceful atmosphere in your bedroom by using bright or soothing colours, flowers, crystals, candles, music, light, incense, herbs, pictures, plants and anything else that makes you feel relaxed and happy.

- Meditation, mantras, prayer and music also aid sleep and dreams.

- Move your bed North, South, West or East and see which position gives you the best dreams. It is said that the bedhead placed North gives the best results, but it is more important to discover what suits you.

- Pillows filled with herbs can induce both sleep and dreams. A dream pillow should be made of cotton or silk, be fairly flat and not measure more than 15 by 12" (38 by 31 cm). Among many recipes, one that is highly effective is a mixture of one part rosemary, lavender and sweet marjoram and half a part of thyme and spearmint. Then add one tablespoon of orris root powder, one tablespoon of dried orange peel and one teaspoon of powdered cinnamon. Mix well and put in the bag, which must be placed under the pillow and slightly to one side so that the warmth from the sleeper's head causes the herbs to exude their fragrance and induce a sound natural sleep and inspirational dreams.

- A recipe for a dream-promoting herbal tisane uses half a tablespoon of fresh or dried rosemary, mixed with one and a quarter cups of cold water, brought to the boil and sweetened with honey. Other useful and powerful herbal sleep inducers are chamomile, Californian poppy, lime blossom and red clover. A mix of one part valerian and one part passion flower made into a tea and drunk last thing at night releases tension and eases one into sleep.

- Leave the day behind. Briefly sum it up and write it down. This will also help dream interpretation. If you hate writing, mentally sum up the day and let it float away in a bath or a shower or by soaking your feet in warm water. Take slow, easy breaths as you do so. If you shower, imagine standing in the rain or under a waterfall – if you can literally do this, even better. If you regret something from your day, forgive yourself (or anyone else) for whatever it may be.

- Relaxation is a key element in sleep and dream preparation, and among the most important methods is control of your breathing. The following technique, which stimulates both dreams and relaxation, is probably the most powerful:

a) Kneel back on your haunches, with both hands resting, palms up.

b) Close your eyes, inhale to the count of six, hold the breath in to the count of six and then exhale to the count of six. Do this sequence at least six times each for maximum benefit, although it can be done as many times as you like.

c) With your eyes still closed, touch the tip of the little finger to the top of the thumb on each hand. Continue the same rhythm of breathing.

d) Extend the little fingers and thumbs, while folding the three middle fingers of each hand into the palms. Continue the in, down and out to count of six breathing.

e) Close all the fingers over the thumb on each hand, making a fist. Continue to breathe as before.

f) Go back to step a) and open your hands, palms up and continue the in, down and out to count of six breathing. Gradually relax into normal breathing. This exercise not only stimulates dreams, but can also be used by people who are sleepless or in great pain. If it is too uncomfortable to kneel, sit in a chair. If you are in bed, lie on your back with your arms resting alongside your body and your hands open, palms upwards. As you practise this, you will notice that the movements of the fingers alter where the air goes in the lungs. Even people who swear they never remember dreams have had almost immediate success after this exercise.

- Crystals are excellent catalysts both for dreaming and remembering your dreams. Put them under the pillow, on a bedside table, on the floor, in the bed or around it. If you decide to use crystals to stimulate dreams, remember that the clearer and more sparkling a crystal is, the more energizing it will be. The more opaque it, or any other gem, is, the more soothing and calming its effect. Amethyst, rose quartz and blue lace agate are good 'sleep-inducers'.

- Make sure you have everything that you need to record your dreams – a pen, pencil, notepad, journal, or tape-recorder, and a torch – beside your bed before you go to sleep. If you awake with a dream

in your head you should record it at once. If you have to search for paper and pen, the dream is likely to vanish.

- Before turning out the light do not forget to write down 'I want to dream and I want to remember my dreams.' Remember that to ask a dream for help, healing or insight is a form of dream incubation and it will work better if you concentrate on it before sleep.

- Another trigger is to set an alarm to wake you every one and a half hours and immediately write down any dream you remember. If you remember nothing, note the first thoughts that come into your mind. Although this course of action is somewhat drastic (and may be unpopular with your sleeping partner!) it works within two or three days and is usually needed only once.

- Vitamin B6 and niacin can be helpful for both dreaming and dream recall. A shortage of B6 – the 'mental vitamin' – makes it difficult to remember dreams and all the B vitamins help counteract stress and emotional imbalance.

All these techniques are simple and effective, and none of them take a lot of time. Pick whichever of these ideas feel right for you, and adapt or develop them to your own needs. You will probably find that one or two work better for you than others. Remember, too, that most of us dream – or remember our dreams – less when tired, overworked or emotionally stressed. Sleeping pills, drugs and alcohol can also interfere with our ability to dream.

How to incubate dreams

The priests, priestesses, wise men and magicians of ancient Greece and Egypt were highly trained in the use of ritual, ceremony and spiritual discipline as part of the preparation for incubating, or inducing dreams. They purified themselves, fasted, prayed, recited special formulae and dozens of incantations to ward off evil and give protection during sleep. To arouse the imagination and induce a sense of euphoria they prepared themselves with ceremonies which included art, music, movement, dance, acting and mime, as well as the use of herbs, incense and intoxicating drugs.

If you are ever in need of insight into a difficult problem, or you desire a special kind of dream, then preparation and ritual can be very useful. A good start is to assemble candles, flowers (especially roses), plants, incense, crystals and stones, favourite objects or colours,

handmade glass, mirrors, pictures that you either love or are inspired by.

All these help to create a sacred atmosphere in a room. Physical preparation can include long walks, sitting against a tree, swimming in the sea – anything that puts you in touch with nature – as well as a fast. You do not have to follow all of these suggestions at once. You may want to take a few days or weeks to prepare, especially if you have reached a crossroads in your life and are seeking answers about where to go next. But the more preparation you put into this, the more powerful the result is likely to be.

After you have prepared yourself in whichever way you prefer, the most simple way to incubate a dream is to write a question down and literally sleep on it by putting it under your

pillow. Write down not only your question on paper but also your own, waking, solution to whatever problem you may have. Think of the pros and cons to these solutions and note them. This clears your subconscious and unconscious mind. You may wish to question your dreaming mind about health, in which case you may want to ask questions such as 'How can I heal myself?', 'What am I meant to learn through this illness?' 'How can I handle pain?', 'How can I deal with the fear of death?' or 'How can I keep my body in an optimum state of health?'

If you have a problem, a decision to make or a relationship question, follow the same principle. When you awake, write down any thoughts and ideas you might have as the result of your dream. If, after a few days, you need greater clarity, write down 'I need greater clarity or deeper understanding' – even if it's a repeat of the dream, and sleep with the paper under your pillow.

If you have never paid attention to your dreams before, you need to let your dreaming mind know that you are now seriously ready to listen.

How to Interpret Your Dreams

Our dreams are the most honest reflection of what we really feel and think about ourselves and life. There are dozens of methods of exploring and integrating dreams into our daily lives.

   The ones I describe here have been used successfully over many years. They work as well with groups as with individuals, and many of them are also suitable for and popular with children.

Eight simple steps to recording and exploring a dream:

1. Give the dream a title
which embodies its essence and which will, on re-reading it, weeks, months or years later, immediately remind you of its story.

2. Describe the main action
such as running away, typing a letter, acting in a play, driving a car… Are these activities common or peculiar to your daily life? If so, why?

3. Note the feelings in the dream
plus, later, your waking feelings about the dream, and how these relate to your daily life, i.e. do you experience the same emotions awake or asleep?

4. Outline the dream setting
is it natural or man-made? A natural setting is one in which forests, mountains, lakes, beaches, parks and gardens appear, while man-made settings include cars, trains, buses, city streets, airports, buildings, computers etc. Does the setting change from one category to the other?

5. Describe the people

and their qualities, plus what part of you or who in your life they remind you of.

6. List the symbols

and objects – especially those that in some way stand out.

7. Sum up in as few words

as possible what the dream appears to be saying.
(Do this spontaneously, intuitively, and without reference to an 'official' dream interpretation book.)

8. Make the dream a reality

by performing in your waking-life the action suggested by the dream's message. To record a dream in this way captures the key points without having to write out the whole story. If you have no time to do more than note down key elements (as in the following example), then later sum up what each aspect of the dream means to you, together with its message.

Title	*White Parrot Dream*
Action	*Running, dancing*
Feelings	*Laughter, freedom, anxiety*
Setting	*Dance-hall*
People	*Boss, next-door neighbour, guard on train*
Symbols	*Parrot, train, shoe, dancers*

The woman who had this dream said that for her the parrot (as in the title) represented love and chatter; the action of running and dancing combined freedom, performance and release; the feeling of laughter and freedom was the past, while anxiety meant stress; the dance-hall was excitement; the boss, authority; the neighbour, a friend; the guard, protection and security; the dancers

were companions. The main symbols of parrot, train, shoe and dancers signified communication, journey, walking and freedom.

The message she took from this dream was to release old memories, face her fear of authority (which was causing her stress) and walk into a new life of love and companionship, knowing she was protected, guarded and guided all the way. She summed up the main message of the dream as 'Freedom.' This dreamer was someone who, although full of fun and humour, had been bullied by father, step-father and husband. She made her dream a reality not by walking away from the stressful situation but by taking small steps to assert her independence, relaxing and having fun. And, despite her husband's disapproval, she also bought two lovebirds! Her life is now much happier.

This is a basic and simple way to record and work with a dream. As you become more proficient, you may want to write down every detail of a dream and explore every minute facet of it. The following questions will all be key to your exploration:

Where is the dream set?

Many of us ignore the dream setting as irrelevant to the main dream story. However, the setting is similar to the backdrop of a theatre stage – it helps set the scene and gives clues for whatever subsequently takes place. According to Jung, 'The description of the locality is very important; the place where the dream is staged, whether hotel, station, street, wood, under water, etc., makes a tremendous difference in the interpretation.'

How do you feel?

Feelings are the most important feature of every dream. We should include in our dream analysis – though not necessarily at the moment of writing the dream down – not only how we feel within the dream but also how we feel awake, about the setting, the people, the events, the actions we make or observe, the objects and symbols that may pop up.

   Dreams pluck from our innermost parts feelings which most of us have learned to suppress, to the point where we do not even know what our true feelings are, and present them to us disguised as pictures, symbols and metaphors. When we translate the images back into feelings we can recognize, we can come to terms with our true emotions, which in turn can lead to a dramatic healing of the psyche.

Mark, a highly successful and somewhat arrogant businessman, dreamed of a man encased in steel-plated armour that threatened to stifle him to death. Mark released the headpiece to find he was face to face with himself. Shocked, he awoke and realized that from the age of eight, when his mother had abandoned him, he had armoured himself against his feelings in order to survive. Before this, Mark had been unaware of how he had stifled his feelings in order to cope with the world around them.

What is happening in the dream?

Dream actions, and especially what we feel about them as we either observe or carry them out, are another indication of what the overall dream theme is trying to communicate. If a dream is so action-packed that there is no time to record every event, we should pick the one or two most bizarre or striking activities and drop the rest. Always look at how dream activities relate to, or contradict, anything in waking life. Question every aspect of a dream from the perspective of a newly arrived alien from another planet.

Dream activities

Amongst the enormous range of activities we get up to in dreams – which can include anything we might have seen, heard of or done in waking-life – some of the most common are:

- being chased
- running away
- falling off cliffs or out of windows, down stairwells, into black holes or dark pools of water
- getting stuck in narrow tunnels or airless caves
- searching for toilets; urinating or defecating in public places
- driving cars, or any other form of transport;

flying, running to catch trains, planes or buses

- dancing on stage or presenting a public lecture and suddenly realizing you are either semi-naked or completely so
- searching for handbags, wallets, money, tickets and passports
- trying to find a way out of a maze of rooms or looking for specific people down corridors that never end.

Look at how comfortable you feel both during and after the dream. Do running, falling or flying give you a sense of exhilaration or panic? If you are involved with a vehicle, are you confident or nervous in the driver's seat, or are you stuck behind it pushing or pulling? If you find yourself naked in front of a crowd of people are you embarrassed or indifferent – and do they notice? If you are searching for a passport, money or hidden jewels, are you excited and expectant or fearful of not finding what you seek? If you are running, are you running away from or towards a person or situation? No matter what our dream activities may be, they mirror what we do in waking-life. If you run away in dreams, there may be something in life you avoid – something you cannot, or will not, face. If you search for lost passports, ID cards, licences, purses, hidden diaries, keys and treasure you may be looking for lost, 'put to one side' buried parts of yourself, as well as for old identities which you need to replace with new ones.

Nightmare activities

Any fear or apprehension we may have awake will be exaggerated in a nightmare. So we run for, but miss the train, plane, bus or very important appointment. We try to run, but cannot, because our feet remain glued to the ground – or our legs will not move because they are encased in mud, cement or water. We may be paralysed from the waist down; we may call for help or give a speech and no sound emerges. We must present information to the government or the news on TV and our notes fly away. Our hair and teeth fall out; our faces crack like broken masks. We forget where we live, or where we parked the car. We drive cars with brakes that suddenly fail; we fly or climb mountains and suddenly fall to earth. We are chased, imprisoned, suffocated, or in some way threatened by such a monstrous figure or overwhelming calamity that we wake up with hearts thumping, gasping for breath, desperate to get away.

   These dreams reflect our anxiety and fear that we will not measure up to or successfully achieve other people's expectations of us. Such dreams are very common to TV announcers, radio presenters, actors and actresses – in fact to anyone performing in public. Aside from indicating an insecurity about what we do, they can also nudge us to prepare better for a particular task.

Overcoming nightmares

The best way of dealing with any form of nightmare or dream threat is to get back into it as quickly as possible and face it. Imagine being in the dream again. Confront the source of anxiety or threat and point your finger or a ray of colour, love or light at it until it shrinks to a manageable size. Remember that you are dealing with emotional energy that is often exaggerated in dreams. Once it is small enough to pick up, hold and question it; 'Who are you? What are you? What part of me do you represent? How can I heal or help you? How can you help me?' Confront and conquer the threat rather than run away from it. If this is not possible within the dream setting, to visualize doing it while awake produces the same result.

Children who are taught to do this with dreams learn that in life, by facing what appears to be a threat, they can shrink it to a manageable size and overcome it.

Dream people

The cast of characters in our dreams – from the mean and nasty to the naughty and nice – highlight good, bad and indifferent parts of ourselves, no matter what secondary meaning they may have. They bring to our attention characteristics we dislike, are unaware of or need to honour and acknowledge. To enter into dialogue with dream people, whether known or unknown in waking-life, can help us explore the dynamics of our everyday relationships.

People in dreams often help us to audition and rehearse for waking-life situations. Dreams in which people's appearance changes dramatically – such as their teeth falling out or their faces crumbling – can indicate a fear of ageing, loss of sexuality or any other kind of attractiveness; or that we are losing our grip on a situation; or the need to let go of any kind of façade regarding how we present ourselves to others; or even that we may need to see a dentist! If we witness a figure who either attacks or kills, or find (within the dream scenario) that we are doing likewise, it usually signifies killing off an aspect of

ourselves that is either destructive and no longer serves our need to grow and develop, or cutting off an influence such as a parent or teacher that we need to move away from.

Jung introduced the idea of archetypes in dreams – universal images that symbolize certain character traits, behaviour and energy patterns. In the past, archetypal figures popped up in our dreams in the shape of gods, goddesses, heroes, wise old men or women, witches, hermits, queens, innocent child and so on. Today's archetypes are more likely to appear in the form of currently popular movie or television stars, politicians, public figures, actors, actresses and even the imaginary heroes and heroines from books. So, well known personalities such as Queen Elizabeth II, Princess Diana, Mother Teresa, George Clooney, Nelson Mandela, Churchill, President Kennedy, Madonna, Marilyn Monroe can all appear as archetypes in our dreams.

Whether you are looking at a king, queen, president, TV announcer, postman, dustman or movie star in your dream, think about why your unconscious has chosen to project that particular image on your dream screen. What is that person doing, saying and feeling, and what is that telling you about yourself?

Dream symbols

We can explore dream symbols, whether living or inanimate, in virtually the same way that we investigate any other parts of the dream. If, say, a hat, a wire coat-hanger and a pair of scissors appear as dream objects, think about whether they fit in with the general theme or seem completely out of place. And why? What associations do these objects have for us in waking-life? Do we use them ourselves? All the time or occasionally? A 'hat' could be seen as 'frivolous' if you associate it with a day at the races, or a champagne picnic. It will mean something completely different if you connect it with mountain skiing or church weddings and funerals. You might associate 'wire coat-hanger' with

'inadequate' or 'inferior' if you prefer padded hangers, or as something to do with dry-cleaners or hotel cloakrooms. Scissors could imply surgery, sewing, cutting through, hair-cut, toe-nails and so on.

In general, living symbols such as animals, flowers and plants relate to the innocent, naïve, natural, childlike parts of ourselves and connect us more deeply with the emotional side of our nature. Flowers symbolize purity, beauty, truth and perfection and lift our spirits. Animals symbolize the animal, instinctive, wild, playful or domesticated side of our nature. To interpret any kind of animal, whether it be bird, beast or fish, look at what it represents to you. The wilder a dream animal is, the more likely it is that the instincts or habits it represents are out of control – especially if it is chasing you. If an animal appears to be abandoned, neglected, starving or in some other way ill-treated, what part of yourself have you also neglected?

Always apply your understanding of the symbol to your life. If you cannot think what significance a particular symbol may have, ask questions of it. 'What are you doing in my dream? What part of me do you represent? Keep questioning until answers begin to pop up. With practice it becomes very easy.

Dream dictionaries

Many people prefer to consult a dream interpretation dictionary rather than take the time to work out their own dream symbology. However, it is quite illogical to imagine that dream symbols have exact and invariable meanings. In one dream seminar I asked the participants to say, in a word or two, what 'bed' implied to them. Among fifty or so different answers, these are some of the words that came up: 'repose', 'escape', 'sex', 'foundation', 'frustration', 'sleep', 'hospital', and so on. Each person had a different association to the word 'bed'. It is also possible that 12 months later their description might completely change. So people who choose to interpret any part of a dream from a dictionary tend to get stuck with a surface meaning of the dream and therefore miss the personal, waking-life material that underlies the dream's real message.

The importance of personal interpretation

Freud once said:

The dreamer does know what his dream means, only he does not know that he knows it and, for that reason, thinks he does not know it.

Many of us would recognise this description. To gain understanding of our dreams we prefer to trust a 'qualified dream expert', the local psychic, a friend or a book – anybody or anything except ourselves. And yet, because a dream is an intimate communication from the soul to the personality, only the dreamer can decipher and truly know their own dreams. Another person's insight may bring us to a deeper or different understanding, but it is coloured by the dreamer's own experience, perception and prejudice.

A dream is an encoded message unique to the dreamer and therefore we must never rest exclusively on someone else's interpretation. No matter how universal dream symbols appear to be, they are an exclusive expression of the person who dreams them and should be interpreted as such.

Antique, for example, may be described in a dream dictionary as meaning 'old, valuable, out of date, past, history'. But for me, antique immediately reminds me of my grandmother's passion for old furniture, auctions and sales-rooms, my grandmother's house, overflowing with antique furniture, and her rage when I spilled ice-cream on a treasured dining-room table. Always think about what the dream's images remind you of. Water will have a totally different meaning and association to a person who drinks a lot of it than to someone who has nearly drowned, for example.

Always record major colours and symbols and see if there is a particular dream theme, colour, symbol or number that corresponds.

Black-and-white dreams tend to be drier – more intellectual – whereas colourful dreams suggest emotion and creativity. Always note the numbers, figures of speech, colours, puns and names in a dream.

Remember that every dream can have two, three or more interpretations or messages, and, by looking at dreams from different angles, we can greatly expand our understanding of them. With any of these exercises do not be afraid of making a mistake. Say to yourself, 'This is the way I currently understand my dream. Tomorrow, next month or next year I may understand it differently.' It is also more important to initially sum up a dream's overall meaning and then look at what we associate with each image, action and feeling than to focus on the literal interpretation of each word.

Knowing the truth of your dream

For Jung the purpose of dream interpretation was the dreamer's psychological development. He suggested four tests to apply to the truth of an interpretation:

1. Does the interpretation 'click' with you?
2. Does the interpretation 'act' for (or give new energy to) you?
3. Is the interpretation confirmed by subsequent dreams?
4. Do the events predicted in a dream occur in waking-life?

And finally …

Dreamwork and dream interpretation should be simple, practical and, above all, fun. Do not let any of the suggestions in this book become a burden, but rather use or adapt what works for you and drop the rest. If there is not enough time to record a dream each day, note the one you still remember two or three days later. Instead of analysing, or working with, every dream, pick one a week or a month or every six months. When a dream hits the spot, when every cell in your body tingles, you will automatically integrate its wisdom into your life.

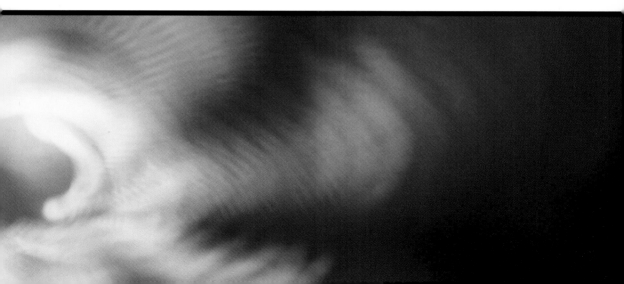

Further Reading
and Useful Addresses

Oneicrocritic
Artemidorus, Original Books, 1991

Jonathan Livingston Seagull
Richard Bach, Pan, 1973

Discipleship in the New Age
Alice Bailey, Lucis Press Trust, 1955

The Orion Mystery
Robert Bauval and Adrian Gilbert, Mandarin, 1995

Keeper of Genesis
Robert Bauval and Graham Hancock, Mandarin, 1997

The Search for Bridie Murphy
Morey Bernstein, Pocket Books, 1978

Saved by the Light
Dannion Brinkley and Paul Perry, Piatkus, 1994

Peace in the Light
—, Piatkus, 1995

De Divinatione
Cicero, Heinemann, 1959

The Projection of the Astral Body
Carrington Hereward and Sylvan Muldoon, Century, 1989

Watch Your Dreams
Ann Ree Colton, ARCPublishing, 1979

Breakthrough Dreaming
Gayle Delaney, Bantam, 1997

The Pierced Priest
Jim Gallagher, Fount, 1995

Fingerprints of the Gods
Graham Hancock, Mandarin, 1996

The Dreaming Brain
J. Allan Hobson, Penguin, 1990

The Holistic Herbal
David Hoffman, Element Books, 1988

The Power of Gems and Crystals
Soozi Holbeche, Piatkus, 1989

The Power of your Dreams
—, Piatkus, 1991

Journeys Through Time
—, Oneicrocritica, Piatkus, 1995

Changes
—, Piatkus, 1997

The Undiscovered Self
C. G. Jung, The Princeton University Press, 1990

**The Hiram Key: Pharaohs, Freemasons
and the Discovery of the Secret Scrolls of Jesus**
Christopher Knight and Robert Lomas, Arrow Books, 1997

Bringers of the Dawn
Barbara Marciniak, Bear and Co., 1993

The Medicine Way
Kenneth Meadows, Element Books, 1990

Confessions of an English Opium Eater
Thomas de Quincey, 1822

The Masters of the Far East
De Vorss &Co., Baird T. Spalding, 1924

The Sirius Mystery
Robert Temple Century, 1998

Pilgrimage to Rebirth
Erla van Waveren, Samuel Weiser, 1991

Autobiography of a Yogi
Yogananda, Paramhansa, Rider, 1946

Association for Research and Enlightenment A.R.E.
PO Box 595, Virginia Beach,
V.A. 23451, USA

Paul Solomon Foundation
620 14th Street, Virginia Beach
V.A.23451, USA

Ann Ree Cotton Orginisation
ARC Publishing, P.O. Box 1138
Glendale, CA. 91209, USA

School of Psychic Studies
16 Queensberry Place
London SW7 2EB, UK